Captain Doris Vail:
Female Navy Trailblazer

A Memoir

CAPTAIN DORIS VAIL: FEMALE NAVY TRAILBLAZER

Copyright © 2020 DORIS VAIL All rights reserved.

All rights reserved. No part of this publication may be reproduced, stored in a retrieval system or transmitted, in any form, or by any means, electronic, mechanical, recorded, photocopied, or otherwise, without the prior written permission of both the copyright owner and the above publisher of this book, except by a reviewer who may quote brief passages in a review. The scanning, uploading, and distribution of this book via the Internet or via any other means without the permission of the publisher is illegal and punishable by law. Please purchase only authorized electronic editions and do not participate in or encourage electronic piracy of copyrightable materials. Your support of the author's rights is appreciated.

Editor: Margaret Best

Cover Photo: U.S. Navy Photograph

Cover Design by Hallard Press LLC/John W Prince

Page Design, Typography & Production by Hallard Press LLC/John W Prince

Published by Hallard Press LLC.

www.HallardPress.com   Info@HallardPress.com   352-234-6099

Bulk copies of this book can be ordered at Info@HallardPress.com

Printed in the United States of America

Library of Congress Control Number: 2020915416

ISBN: 978-1-951188-11-5

To my family and friends
who urged me
to write my story.

Table of Contents

Introduction	vi
Early Life	3
Why The Navy	13
Newport Rhode Island OCS	17
Communication Command Center	29
Naval Air Station, North Island California	35
RTC Recruit Training Center, Bainbridge, Maryland	49
NAVSTA Rota, Spain	57
Naval Station, Anacostia	63
Washington DC	69
Industrial College of the Armed Forces ICAF	75
Enlisted Strength Plans Division	79
Deputy Director of OP-12	83
Capt. Doris Vail Retires	87
Vail Retires From Navy	93
After The Navy	97
The Ranch	103
International Women Veterans Golf Association	103
The Women's Memorial	107
Personal Life	111
Momma and Daddy	113
Family Serving America	118
Yearly Bicycle Rides	123
Fort Lauderdale Airport Shooting	129
Villages Life	135
Trailblazer Firsts	137
About The Author	139
List of Research	141

INTRODUCTION

Life for women in the military, in the 50s and 60s, was difficult, but I persevered. As a trailblazer, I became the first woman in many positions, creating openings for women in the service today. Because of my involvement in discussions at headquarters and my tenacity in writing regulations showing how to adapt ships for female Sailors, congress changed the role of Women In the Navy (WIN).

The Navy now assigns women to jobs not previously open to them. The service academies are open to interested female officers. Women can now join male Sailors on ships, become mechanics, and command both male and female companies during times of peace and war. Promotions are easier to come by, and life in the service has improved.

My friends and family ask about my life as a female Naval officer, often saying, "You should write a book." I wrote this book not only for my nieces and nephews but also for any woman who wishes to become a female naval Sailor or a WIN today.

The Navy now differs from what it was when I joined. Many restrictions placed on WAVEs or Woman Accepted for Volunteer Service have, over time, changed. We are now Women In the Navy known as WINs. I am proud to have been part of these changes.

I hope to show you how through faith, strength, duty, luck, and hard work, many women and I blazed the trail, so all women who join the Navy are granted equal privilege and responsibility as their male counterparts. People call me a trailblazer, but I only did my duty to the best of my ability, so others who follow can do theirs.

— Captain Doris R. Vail (US Navy Ret.)

Captain Vail: Female Navy Trailblazer

Cheyenne, Wyoming (Used with permission Gunhild Hexamer)

1.
Early Life
Doris Vail

At six years old, in Cheyenne, Wyoming, rheumatic fever, and St. Vitus Dance seemed to appear out of nowhere. When my hands started shaking, and I could not move my food to my mouth and dropped glasses of water, Momma took me to the doctor. He insisted she take me to Children's Hospital in Denver for a proper diagnosis.

Rheumatic Fever accounted for many childhood deaths during the 40s. The illness caused by untreated strep throat or scarlet fever infections could develop into heart problems. Mine became a general infectious response to my immune system. Today, penicillin cures childhood rheumatic fever, but there was no cure in rural Wyoming in 1940.

My family, known as the "five Ds," settled in Wyoming when I was a baby. I grew up in Cheyenne with my older brother, Dexter, and older sister, Donna. Daddy, named

Donald, worked for the Union Pacific Railroad, and Momma, Dorothy, stayed home.

Momma's brother's sister-in-law, Oma, a retired nurse living in Denver, agreed to care for me, allowing Momma's return to Cheyenne to watch over Dexter and Donna. While living with Oma, I received medical care at the Children's Hospital.

Oma's daughter, Jonnie May, lived with her and worked long hours at the telephone company. Neither Oma nor Jonnie May celebrated Christmas or birthdays as they were members of Jehovah's Witness religion. Momma made sure I received both Christmas and birthday presents. She often visited for my doctor appointments and hospitalizations. I stayed with Oma for three years from 1941 to 1944.

Oma attempted to enroll me in the public school system, but it did not accept me. I missed the second, third, and fourth grades. Every day, Oma and I walked the dog in the park, giving strength to my legs. I attended Bible Study and went door-to-door, passing out Jehovah's Witness pamphlets and answering questions. Jonnie May taught me to read music and play the piano while I learned to read during Bible lessons with Oma. I missed my family and friends and school.

During those formative years, I developed independence and strength in character, knowing my parents cared enough to give me the proper medical help, a caring foster family, and visits. I returned home to Cheyenne after a doctor's appointment with Momma. The doctor gave her a letter I did not read.

The Five "Ds" Donna, Doris, Donald, Dorothy, Dexter Vail at their home in Cheyenne, Wyoming. 1943

Doris Vail

Doris, dog and Oma
1941-1944

Jonnie May

Momma said, "You have to go home with me now." Tired of living with Oma and happy to return to my family, I thanked Oma for her care and Jonnie May for teaching me to play the piano. Momma and I returned to Cheyenne.

Dexter, Donna, and Daddy embraced me. We ate a wonderful meal together and caught up on all our happenings. My mother tried to enroll me in school, but the doctor said I was too ill, so my brother and sister tutored me in mathematics until Dexter left to serve in the Navy.

A miracle drug called penicillin became available, so the doctor in Cheyenne gave me shots. No one knew what would result from these shots. He came to our house every four hours and gave me a shot of penicillin in my rear. After a time, he announced I was well enough to attend school. Momma allowed me to read the letter from the doctor in Denver.

The letter stated I would die in six months. The doctor thought my mother should take me home so I could die with my family. I had become nine-years-old. The letter shocked me. I thanked the Lord for keeping me alive and promised him I would be good. Reading the letter became a significant experience for me.

Momma tried once again to enroll me in school. I entered sixth grade in 1946 because the school system philosophy was to keep the children with their age group. I could read, but I lacked spelling, vocabulary, writing, and math skills appropriate to the sixth grade. I knew nothing about multiplication or division. My mother, teacher, brother, and sister spent time with me every day helping with my lessons. Through a lot of determination, perseverance, and extra study, I excelled in school, even though I had missed grades 2 to 5.

In 1946, Momma and Daddy bought a ranch with a log cabin built in 1899. It needed lots of work. There was no inside water or electricity. A wood-burning stove provided heat and a hearth for cooking. Grandad Jake, my mother's father, and my Uncle Byrle lived on a small farm outside Cheyenne. When I told Grandad Jake, I would spend my summers with him on the ranch, he nearly jumped for joy.

My parents, brother, and sister worked in Cheyenne during the summers, so I joined Grandad Jake on the ranch where he taught me how to cook on the woodstove and drive a team of horses. We had an outhouse, a spring for drinking water, and used Coleman lanterns for light. I grew healthy, carrying water for washing from a nearby spring. I helped with plowing, planting, and harvesting. As the years progressed, we bought a tractor and combine. I greased the combine because Grandad Jake did not fit under it. He taught me safety and how to shoot the .22 long rifle, killing porcupines, prairie dogs, and badgers. I felt like a pioneer and loved every minute.

In 1948, crews traveled from farm to farm harvesting crops. When they came to our farm, I drove the truck picking up the hay bundles they gathered. At noon I returned to the cabin and prepared lunch for all the workers. Being out in nature, working hard, and loving every minute brought me joy.

Dorothy and Don Vail at The Ranch, 1993.

Living with Grandad Jake and working with and learning from him brought both of us happiness. Because he fixed and drank a cocktail every evening, but didn't like to drink alone, he allowed me to drink one with him. I liked bourbon and 7-up, but I was too young to drink, so I never over imbibed. Grandad Jake saw to that.

We rode horses every night, often traveling three miles visiting our neighbor where we would pick up milk and butter and sometimes share a meal with them. I became more self-sufficient, able to solve problems, and resilient during my time at the ranch.

Momma and Daddy purchased a house on the other side of Cheyenne in 1947 when I started junior high, allowing me to get to the school every day more easily. I took music lessons on the string base. By the time I was in high school, the 10th -12th grades, I had progressed to playing in the concert orchestra and the dance band. I also attended a week at the music school in Snowy Range, Wyoming, where we slept in sleeping bags on the ground every night. Every morning, at sunup, we played music, then learned music theory. At the end of that week, we performed at the University of Wyoming in Laramie to a considerable audience. They transmitted the concert throughout the state by radio.

During my senior year, I played solo on the string base, winning first place at the State Music Fair in the State Music Festival in Casper, Wyoming. The University of Wyoming offered me a full four-year music scholarship where I would

Captain Vail: Female Navy Trailblazer

Doris playing string base at Music Camp Snowy Range.

teach and play with other string base musicians and take classes. I turned the opportunity down because I didn't want to go to the same school as my sister. People compared me to her and wanted me to emulate her, but I wanted to be myself.

Through a lot of additional studies, I stayed in school and graduated from high school with my class in May 1953. During my last two years of high school, I worked as a soda jerk in a drug store in Cheyenne. Through all these experiences, I developed into an independent, self-sufficient, well-adjusted young woman.

I attended the University of Denver from September 1953 to May 1958. At first, I took special classes in spelling, vocabulary, and speed reading. I joined the Sigma Kappa Sorority during my first year in school. They elected me treasurer of the sorority the second year in school and elected me the president of Iota chapter of Sigma Kappa in my third year at university.

I joined the Sigma Kappa Sorority President's Conference in Ohio and rode the bus from Denver, changing buses along the way. I rode on, but my luggage did not, so I arrived with no clothing. My sorority sisters loaned me clothing and items from their baggage. My luggage arrived the day I was to leave. I learned much about the feeling of togetherness and sisterhood while being a member of that sorority.

I earned my Bachelor of Arts Degree in special education. After four years of teacher training, I served my student teaching at Boetcher School for Crippled Children.

2.
Why
The Navy?

Never in my wildest dreams did I think about joining the Navy. My brother, Dexter, had served after the Second World War. He served a three-year term on what was called a "kiddie cruise." He attended electronic schools and sailed on one ship to Alaska. No one in my family served during the Korean Conflict, so the military was not part of my family's experience.

Besides, we lived in Cheyenne, Wyoming. The only time I saw an ocean was.... well... never.

I spent four years at the University of Denver, studying special education. Was that where I belonged? Certainly not the military. As it turned out, not in special education either.

At twenty-three, I walked into the student union at the university just before graduation in May 1958. There, sitting at the table under a recruitment poster, sat the most beautiful woman in a gorgeous blue uniform. I approached her and said, "I want to join."

Smiling and looking into my eyes, she said, "Don't you want to know about the program?"

"No," I said. "I just want to join."

I had studied special education for physically disabled children, but I was uncertain if I could handle the emotional feelings I had for these children daily. When I saw this lady, I knew I wanted to wear the same uniform and become a naval officer, so, just like that, I joined the Navy to attend Officer Candidate School or OCS.

After graduation, I returned home to Cheyenne while waiting for the OCS class to begin. Honesty is the best policy, I thought.

"Dad," I said. "I joined the Navy."

Mother accepted my announcement, but Dad was less accepting.

"No," he said. "Women don't join the Navy."

He and I fished, tap-danced, and hung out together. I needed to convince him of my decision.

"Dexter joined the Navy," I told him.

Dad retorted, "War is no place for a woman."

"We're not at war, Dad. I'll be a WAVE doing clerical work, nowhere near any war. This is a chance of a lifetime. I'll see the world, do exciting, adventurous things," I responded.

He thought a minute, then shook his head, "No, no. I hear women in the service are loose."

Captain Vail: Female Navy Trailblazer

I put my hand on his shoulder, my eyes pleading for understanding. "That's ridiculous. Don't you trust me? Besides, I've already taken the oath and committed to a few years in the Navy."

He hugged me. "I only want what is good for you."

The day Dad drove me to the airport to catch my flight to Newport, Rhode Island, he hugged me again.

3.
Newport Rhode Island Naval Base Women Officer Candidate School 1958

Newport Naval Base in Rhode Island, the site of the Women's Officer Candidate School (OCS), was flanked by the Navy on all sides. Looking it over, I thought, "You're in the Navy now." On one side of this harbor, I watched Naval ships coming and going. On the other, uniformed senior officers trained for higher commands. Enlisted, civilian, and officer personnel moved from building to building going about their jobs. We women recruits were about to attend sixteen weeks of training to become WAVEs or Women Accepted for Volunteer Emergency Service.

The Navy assigned us, thirty-five female recruits, to a company and barracks. During the first two months, we wore enlisted uniforms with the rating of E-2 (Seaman Apprentice), second from the bottom of the enlisted ratings. We slept together in the barracks, ate together in the enlisted mess hall, did calisthenics, learned Naval history, and studied the Blue Book. The Blue Book explained everything we needed to know about the Navy, how to march, and proper Naval etiquette. Because WAVEs could not be in combat positions, we were not trained with artillery or guns.

Women have always served our country in varying roles. In 1811, when the naval hospital system was established, a young surgeon named William C. Barton lobbied the Navy to staff its new medical establishment with female nurses. During the Civil War, for example, more than a dozen Sisters of the Holy Cross and five African-American women served as nurses aboard the USS Red Rover, a former Confederate steamer captured by the Union Navy and transformed into the first Navy hospital ship.

After the victory in the 1898 Spanish-American War, thousands of soldiers suffered and died from diseases such as malaria, typhus, yellow fever, and dysentery. The military hired 1,563 contract nurses to serve in Cuba, Puerto Rico, Hawaii, and the Philippines, including the hospital ship Relief. Six nurses, including Esther V Hasson, cared for these troops. Esther became the first superintendent of the Navy Nurse Corps.

After years of debate, the Navy Nurse Corps was established on 13 May 1908. The first women to serve as members of the United States Navy became known as "The Sacred Twenty." By 1917, during World War I, the Nurse

Captain Vail: Female Navy Trailblazer

First Superintendent of the Navy Nurse Corps, from 18 August 1908 to 10 January 1911. Official US Navy Photograph, now in the collections of the National Archives.

Corps included 160 women stationed as far away as the Philippines, Guam, and Samoa.

Fortunately, the 1916 law establishing the United States Naval Reserve Force (USNRF) did not specify the reservists had to be men. On 19 March 1917, women who enrolled in the reserve were trained to take over many of the non-fighting positions so men could join the war. Unfortunately, the Naval Appropriations Act of 1919 stipulated all-female reservists, except nurses, be placed on inactive duty within 30 days. The Navy honorably discharged or gave civil service jobs to these women. It was another 23 years before women returned to general service.

During World War II, Navy nurses served on ships and in Hawaii during the Pearl Harbor bombing and on Guam when the Japanese captured the island and took five nurses as prisoners.

Of the twelve nurses captured from Cañacao Naval Hospital in the Philippines, Ann Bernatitus escaped and set up hospitals on the Bataan Peninsula and the island of Corregidor before fleeing the Japanese on a submarine. She became the first to receive the Navy's new Legion of Merit Medal.

Secretary of the Navy William Franklin "Frank" Knox set a plan in motion to form the Women's Reserve. An eight-person Women's Advisory Council selected Mildred Helen McAfee to be the Women's Reserve's first director. She created the acronym WAVES—Women Accepted for

Captain Vail: Female Navy Trailblazer

Lieutenant Junior Grade Ann Bernatitus, Navy Nurse Corps, circa 1943. She was the first recipient of the US Navy Medal of Merit for her work. (Photo source: National Museum of the US Navy.)

(Inset) The US Navy Medal of Merit.

Volunteer Emergency Service. On 30 July 1942, President Franklin Roosevelt signed Public Law 689, creating the Women's Reserve, and McAfee was sworn in as "an office and gentlemen of the United States Navy and received her commission as lieutenant commander — the first female officer of the Naval Reserve.

I felt proud to be part of such a storied history. The Navy placed restrictions on women. No more than five percent of the Naval forces were women. Climbing in the ranks was slow and controlled. Professional gains for Navy women were few during the 1950s and 1960s. About ninety percent of regular and reserve Navy women served in administrative or nursing roles. I enlisted in this restrictive environment. Little did I know of the changes about to occur and the part I would play.

In 1953, Secretary of Defense George Marshall convened a group of distinguished civilian women into a committee called The Defense Advisory Committee on Woman in the Service, or DACCOWITS tasked to improve female recruitment. I did not know it at the time I enlisted, but I became an advisor to the group.

In 1967 Congress opened the path for women to become admirals. On 26 April 1972, President Richard Nixon approved the selection of the first woman to admiral. On 26 April 1972, Alene Duerk became the first female admiral.

Admiral Zumwalt, for whom I worked later in my career, changed and updated Navy policies, including those

Captain Vail: Female Navy Trailblazer

Lieutenant Commander Mildred H. McAfee, USNR while serving as Director of the WAVES.
Photo #: 80-G-K-13616-A80

Rear Admiral Alene B. Duerk, NC, USN

for women. In 1970, he concluded, "female talent is being underutilized."

In 1972, Navy Secretary John Warner authorized a pilot program providing Navy scholarships for women. Admiral Zumwalt wrote memos called Z-Grams, particularly Z-116, improving retention and more significant opportunity for Women In the Navy.

In 1974, a woman earned her wings, and in 1978 women began being assigned duty on ships. I wrote many of the regulations and recommendations for this change in attitude. But at the time I was in OCS, none of this was in my line of sight.

By the time I retired in 1980, I was next in line for promotion to admiral. I had served well and saw many positive changes to the history of Woman In the Navy. But more was to come.

In 2020, at the time of this writing, nearly twenty percent of the entire US Naval Force is female. Women serve on ships, in submarines, and war zones. They command companies and are fully integrated into a once male organization. The first female four-Star Admiral, Michelle Howard, retired in 2017.

The first step for a Woman In the Navy is to enroll, which I did in 1958.

After the first two months of OCS school, we continued our lessons during officer candidate school. We purchased our officer uniforms, learned more regulations, history, and duties. Most of the women talked about their futures and having their parents attend the graduation ceremony. Spirits were high. The day before the commissioning, an officer called me out of class

I stood at attention before the commanding officer. "Seaman Vail," she said. "You will not be graduating with your class. There has been a discrepancy with your records. You are to report to the Naval hospital in Boston."

Little did I know the thyroid surgery I had when a student at Denver University would prohibit me from becoming an officer. After three days in the hospital and many tests, the doctors cleared me to return to OCS and complete my training.

"Seaman Vail," my CO said. "I haven't heard from the hospital. I will allow you to attend class but not to march with them. Do not eat with them until you are commissioned."

What could I do? I was in the Navy now. Orders are orders, and protocol must be kept. Although I still slept in the same barracks with my classmates, I ate alone in the enlisted mess, saluted my friends as they passed by, and carried on for two weeks. Until an officer on the staff called me into the commander's office. She commissioned me as O-1, ensign. I proudly placed my bar and epaulets on my officer's uniform.

I looked sharp in my white Navy uniform with gold ensign bars. The Navy had commissioned the New York fashion house of Mainbocher to design our uniforms back in 1942. The design has not changed much over the years. It is still quite" natty," as one may say.

Our winter uniform is made from navy blue wool and worn with a six-gored blue skirt. The jacket is single-breasted and unbelted. Our summer uniform is white and made from a lighter fabric. The uniform is not complete without our brimmed hat, gloves, black or white pump shoes, shirt, and tie. Oh my, there is nothing like a uniform to make you feel secure, proud, and patriotic.

My commanding officer and my classmates congratulated me for the way I had maintained decorum during those two weeks. Appointed as leader of the class, I marched the entire class around the inside of the graduation room. We performed several military drills for the audience. Many of the candidate's parents were in attendance. Mine was not.

4.
Communication Command Center San Diego, California

The Navy sent me to the Communications and Command Center in San Diego, California, as my first duty station. I, a newly minted ensign, drove alone from Rhode Island to California and reported for duty.

The Communication and Command Center at the foot of Broadway and Harbor Drive in downtown San Diego received and disseminated communications worldwide from and to all Naval operations, ships, and commands. I was responsible for a group of enlisted men, mostly expert communication people, and a room full of equipment used to receive orders and responses. Much of the information received was classified. It was our responsibility to ensure the right commands received the correct information, and the responses went to the proper places.

Our work shifts, called watches, followed a schedule—

three days from 7 am to 3 pm (example Monday–Wednesday), three days from 3 pm to midnight (Thursday-Saturday), and three days from midnight to 7 am (Sunday-Tuesday). Seventy-two hours off before the watches started over again.

Other watches alternated with mine. For example, a women officer would start her watch with her own crew when my watch was over. I was the only officer on the watches except for the day (7a.m. to 3p.m.) when male officers, senior to me, used the time for training or checking on my work. Getting used to working such hours and eating at different times each day required effort for two weeks before it became routine.

The enlisted men and I talked during the midnight shift. We shared our love for music. Several of the men played instruments. One night they agreed to play a little melody. One man brought his guitar, another his piano bar, and a third carried a saw. The sound was pleasing, so I admitted I played a string base in high school and college.

One evening one man presented a rented string base. I joined the group. We discussed having a jam session during our off time. Since I was an officer, "fraternizing" with enlisted was not permitted. I could have been discharged or reprimanded.

I remember the afternoon we got together in one of their homes. We were not on duty. It was hot, so we opened all the windows and doors. Our music rang through the air, and a large gathering of people brought their lawn chairs and listened to us play.

Captain Vail: Female Navy Trailblazer

Medals won with the Women's Rifle Team 11th Naval District.

Our work always came first, but during our seventy-two hours off I enjoyed playing music, sightseeing, or sunbathing on the beach. I joined the Women's Rifle Team at the 11th Naval District, just south of San Diego. Grandad taught me to shoot his .22 rifle, so I was familiar with a gun. I learned to carry the gun and ammunition belt as if it were a war rifle, and how to shoot from three positions—standing, sitting, and lying prone. I competed against Lady Marines from Camp Pendleton and other WAVES from other naval rifle teams winning three medals, but I didn't stay long with the rifle team.

I also enjoyed fishing and gambling on my seventy-two hours off. I'd drive over the border to Tijuana, Mexico, where I walked the streets enjoying the scenes and talked with locals. Often strangers asked to buy me drinks and sit to talk. Luckily, most spoke English. Sometimes they invited me on a short fishing expedition.

Life in the Navy so far seemed like a perfect fit. I held responsibilities, stayed physically fit, and mentally challenged. For a young woman like me, there can be no better life.

Captain Vail: Female Navy Trailblazer

Doris shooting in 1960.

4.
Naval Air Station, North Island, California

I received orders for my second duty station at Naval Air Station (NAS) North Island, California. From 1960 through 1962, I was the only female officer in the command. I became responsible for one-hundred enlisted female sailors in one barracks. The CO (Commanding Officer) and the XO (Executive Officer) held me accountable for everything the enlisted female Sailors did or did not do.

A CO, or commanding officer, is the head person in charge of a military unit. The CO can be of any officer rank, most often a senior officer like an O-5 (commander) and above. An XO or executive officer is the commanding officer's assistant, usually of a lower rank such as an O-4 (lieutenant commander) and above.

The XO called me into his office. "One of your enlisted

got pregnant. How did this happen?"

I'm sure he knew how that happened, but he wanted someone to blame for her misconduct. I couldn't be with every one of my women every minute of the day to police their actions, so I learned to keep my mouth shut.

During the sixties, pregnant WAVEs and homosexual women received honorable or dishonorable discharges. Naval Regulations prohibited married women and those with dependent children from enrolling. The laws changed in 1973, allowing pregnant women to remain in the service should they wish. The ban on gay men and women remained in force until 1993.

A witch hunt mentality prevailed during the McCarthy era of the fifties into the sixties. This witch hunt resulted in less than honorable discharges for women thought to be homosexual. She had no recourse. The XO held me responsible when someone reported one of my women as gay.

"You should have turned them in yourself," he barked.

I attended each investigation performed by the NIS (Naval Investigative Service) as they questioned my women. I knew there was a two-way mirror in the room and a microphone in the desk drawer, so every time the interrogator left the room, I placed my back to the mirror and whispered, "Keep your mouth shut. Don't give the names of the women. Don't answer questions without counsel." I may have saved many careers. I spent hours on end in the interrogation room, protecting my enlisted.

Captain Vail: Female Navy Trailblazer

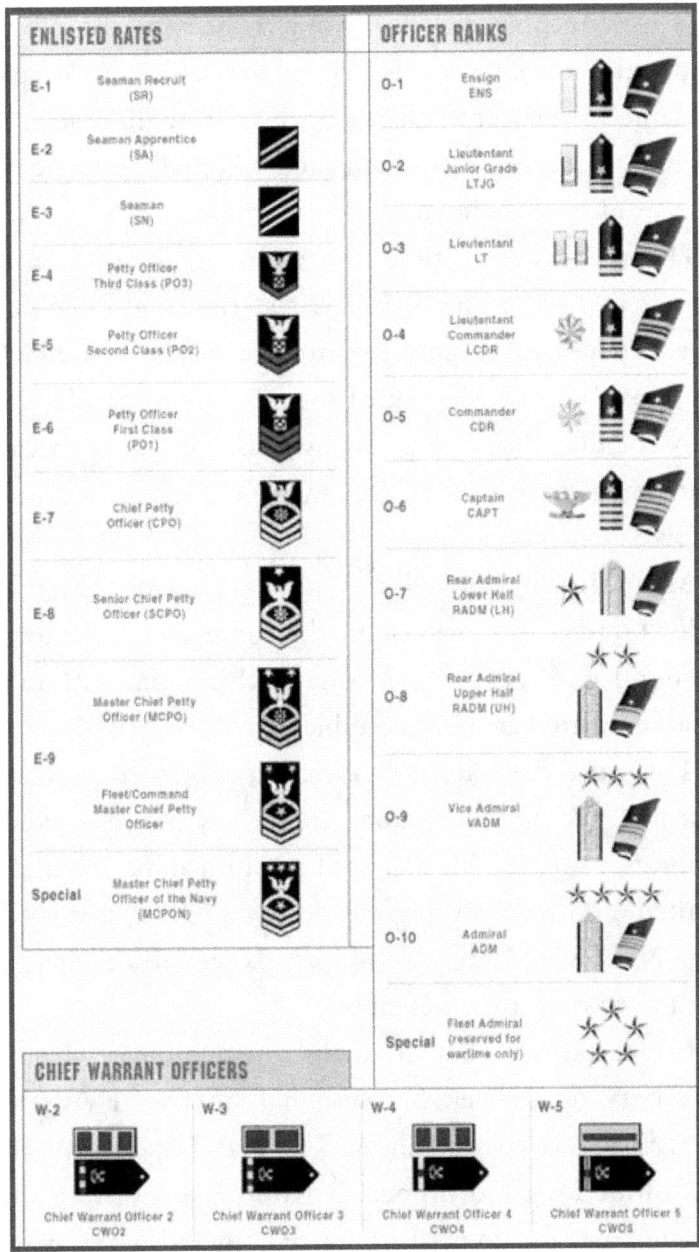

With nothing to do, women become bored, so I volunteered to help those who lived in the barracks keep busy. I became the officer in charge of their softball, baseball, and bowling teams. I also coached the basketball team. I enjoyed every minute of their games—win or lose.

During this same time, the CO told me to attend the Navy Wives Club luncheon. I sat at the head table next to the guest speaker because I wanted to talk to her. The CO's wife "pulled rank." She came to me and said, "You have to go sit by the door because we sit by rank." It was apparent she meant each woman sat by the rank of her husband using it as her own.

My uniform showed the rank of Lt.j.g. (Lieutenant Junior Grade). No one else in the room was in uniform, so I responded, "I am the only one in this room with rank." I remained seated at the head table.

The next day, the CO called me into his office and informed me I would not attend any more wives club meetings. I suppose his wife spoke to him about the incident. I smiled. I didn't want to go to those meetings, anyway. I was not a Navy wife. I was a full-blown Naval officer. It was not my duty to join the wives club.

I maintained contact with my roommate from the University of Denver. She and her boyfriend visited and wanted to go deep-sea fishing. The man I was dating rented an 18-foot long motorboat. Early in the morning, before the sun rose, the four of us started toward Mexican water.

We passed several islands before stopping at one of them and purchasing a bushel barrel of live crabs to be eaten later. We fished throughout the day, surrounded by other fishing boats. We caught huge yellowtail trout, drank beer, and ate our sandwiches. Around 4 pm, we decided to return to San Diego, but the motor would not start.

We looked around for help from those we had seen fishing, but everyone was gone. We saw no other boats. Our boat simply would not start. We checked the gas gage; it was full.

None of us knew what to do. The tide changed and carried us further offshore. You'd think since I was in the Navy, I'd know what to do, but I did not. As we drifted, we noticed an island in the not too far distance. No human lived on that island—just rattlesnakes. We watched the ocean hitting the rocks around that island, knowing we would eventually drift that way.

Darkness fell, so we could no longer navigate by sight. There was no radio on board, so we had no way to contact help. We ladies became seasick. Our boyfriends didn't know what to do. One of them took our flashlight and attached it to the end of a fishing pole, stood in the boat, and waved it into the air. Our boat drifted closer and closer to the island of rattlesnakes. If we hit the rocks surrounding that island, the boat may crash. Aside from being miserably seasick, I shook with fear. Am I more afraid of the water, or rattlesnakes?

I saw a light coming toward us. Would we be rescued?

Slowly, we noticed a big fishing boat behind that light. When they stopped to pull us alongside, I spoke with the captain of that trawler. Sixty fishermen on that boat were headed toward San Diego from Acapulco but had gone off course. If they had stayed on course, they would not have seen us. The captain of the fishing boat said we had twenty minutes before we'd hit the rocks.

Three of us boarded the rescue fishing boat, while my date stayed with our rented motorboat. The captain tied a rope to the little boat and towed it to the Coast Guard ship at the head of the bay in San Diego. The ship was docked at Pt Loma which was a base. I called my roommate and asked her to drive down and pick us up.

She did, but they would not let her on the base to get us because no woman could enter after 10 pm. We waited, drinking coffee, and recovering from our seasickness.

At 5 am, my roommate picked us up and drove back to our shared apartment. My friends cared for themselves while I took a shower, donned my uniform, and reported to the office for duty.

Unusual for me, I sat at my desk, closed my eyes, and nearly fell asleep, when one of the enlisted who worked for me asked what had happened to me. I told her. She entered the lieutenant's office.

He came out of his office, laughing. "Why are you here?"
I looked up through dull eyes, "I have no more leave time."
"Well, you do now. Go home. Get some rest."

My ex-roommate from Denver and her boyfriend had just awakened and were planning to leave when I arrived home about noontime. We packed the fish we caught in ice so she could take them back to Denver with her, said goodbye, and I slept for hours.

The fear and seasickness I felt during that fishing trip took its toll on me, but I thank God He was watching and kept me going for some reason I did not yet understand. The fish did not get away, but this is the fish story, I tell my friends.

I worked at North Island but lived in San Diego, so I rode the ferry to work every day. My parents visited me there. Daddy wanted to go deep-sea fishing, so I took them to the base where the Navy fishing ship operated. I paid $3.00 for each of us. We left early in the morning, anticipating a happy day fishing. Daddy fished regularly and needed no help, but the Sailors onboard the boat insisted on putting the bait on the hook and taking the fish from the hook.

Daddy did not understand the Sailors were only following orders. He thought they were treating him like an older man, so we did not go fishing again. We did, however, spend quality time together in San Diego and on base. This visit became the first of many. Dad accepted my decision about joining the service. After only two days, they returned to Cheyenne, where Daddy resumed working for the railroad, and Mama cared for my father's stepfather, we called Uncle Rollie and Dad's mother, Madge.

Uncle Rollie, my father's stepfather and brother of

Daddy's birth father, had been a bread delivery man in Flint. Michigan. Uncle Rollie and Grandma Madge could no longer live alone, so my brother, Dexter, my sister's husband, Frank, and Daddy moved Uncle Rollie and Madge into an apartment upstairs in Momma and Daddy's home in Cheyenne.

While on leave over Thanksgiving, I had driven Uncle Rollie and Grandma Madge from Cheyenne, Wyoming, to California so they could visit with Aunt Jean, Uncle Rollie's sister. Because I had to report to work immediately, I did not stay with them. When Uncle Rollie and Grandma Madge were ready to return to Cheyenne, Daddy and Momma had to drive to California and return with them to Cheyenne. The four of them lived together, caring for each other.

After Momma and Daddy left my house from his fishing trip and our visit, I had the rest of the year before Christmas at North Island. An enlisted third-class WAVE, from Denver, worked for me in my office. When I prepared to go on leave to Cheyenne for Christmas, I agreed to drop her off in Denver. After doing so, I continued to Cheyenne with the promise of picking her up on the way back to North Island.

I spent a wonderful week at home with my family in Cheyenne. On the day of my leaving to pick up my third-class WAVE, it started to snow. What is a little snow in Wyoming at Christmastime? No big deal.

By the time I arrived in Denver, the snow had become a blizzard. We decided to continue through the snow, but by the time I reached just south of Denver, visibility was poor, the snow mounted, and roads became slippery. We stopped in Walsenburg, Colorado, and attached chains to our tires before continuing to the border with New Mexico. Snow kept falling, and winds became fierce. I stopped at the highway patrol office. I asked if Raton Pass, the road we had to take to get to California, was open.

"No," the trooper said.

But I am stubborn, so without mentioning this to my companion, I returned to the car, started it up, and continued driving. The wind blew hard; the windshield wipers did not touch the windshield. I should have paid attention to that signal, but, as I said, I am stubborn.

Visibility was poor; I could not see far ahead. Conditions were nearly white-out, so we rolled our windows down, stuck our heads out, and carefully watched as I inched my way through the raging storm. The mountain roads curved this way and that. I could not see the middle line. Luckily no other cars had dared the drive.

"There's a light," I pointed toward a small light on the side of the road. "I think that means to turn right."

I turned right. The car stopped. I backed up, hit the gas again. The car would not move.

I left the safety of my automobile, walked outside to see why the car stopped. I had been attempting to drive through a massive snowbank on the side of the mountain. If I had been able to plow through it, we would have slid down the slope. Someone would have found us in the spring with the snowmelt. It was a long way down that cliff.

By this time, the wind had abated a little, the snow and wind calmed a bit. I turned the car to the left and continued to Raton. When we entered the town, I stopped at a gas station and asked for directions to a hotel that may let us stay for a few hours. We had no money. The time was one- in- the- morning.

A policeman led us to a small college in the area and arranged for us to stay for a few hours in one of the empty dorm rooms. "Don't take anything. Stay for a few hours only," he said.

We lay down and rested for about three hours before taking off again. The snow had stopped, but the roads were so icy, I could not drive more than 15 mph. The chains were still hugging the tires. That drive was worse than terrible. When we entered the Arizona state line, the snow turned to slush, then icy water. We removed the chains, and I drove through flooded water on slippery roads. The young WAVE and I remained tense as we crept our way to San Diego.

I deposited the WAVE in her barracks, then went to my home where I slept for a few more hours. I woke up, still asleep, talking on the phone. I recall telling the person on the phone, I was fine, and my parents were with me in California. I had not had enough sleep and was so tired I had become confused.

I dressed in my uniform, knowing I had to be on duty. Still woozy from lack of rest, I told my boss the story of my

Captain Vail: Female Navy Trailblazer

Grandma Madge and Uncle Rollie.

trip.

"Why didn't you call and request a delay in coming in for work?" he said.

I was so new to the military; I did not know I had the option.

When I spoke with my parents, Momma said she had worried about me. "I heard on the news," she said. "Three-hundred-and-fifty cars were stuck on the roadside unable to move during the storm. I thought you were in one of those cars."

Once again, I thanked God for watching over me.

Later that year, the Catholic chaplain and I developed a friendship. We ate lunch together at the Officer's Club, enjoying conversation. The bartender had the chaplain's drink waiting for him every day, so I also ordered a drink. Before long, the bartender placed our glasses side by side, waiting for us at lunchtime.

One day in April 1962, I stepped off the barstool and screamed in pain. The chaplain helped me walk and took me to the doctor. I was diagnosed with a double hernia in my groin and sent to the Balboa Naval Hospital for surgery. I was told after the surgery to rest for at least six weeks, but when I got home, I received orders to Recruit Training Command in Bainbridge, Maryland.

I had travel time and leave time before reporting to my next station. I was going to stay in San Diego for a while to rest, but I received word Uncle Rollie had died of a brain aneurysm on 2 April, so I left immediately driving by myself to Cheyenne so I could be with my Grandmother Madge. I stayed with Grandma for a week and went to Uncle Rollies' funeral.

Grandma and Uncle Rollie had a talking pet parrot. It also flew free in the apartment. The bird sat beside Grandma, saying, "Where is Rollie? Where is Rollie?"

Grandma ignored the bird, but I kept repeating, "Rollie is gone. Don't look for Rollie. Rollie is gone." The bird looked and looked for Rollie. He had been trained to eat out of Rollie's hand, so I offered him his food from my hand. Amazing bird. I left within a week, so maybe he's saying, "Doris, Where is Doris?"

Momma worked, so Grandma had the house to herself during the daytime and seemed to be getting along well. I had received orders for my third duty station in Bainbridge, Maryland, so I left Cheyenne and drove across the country to Maryland.

5.
Recruit Training Command RTC Bainbridge, Maryland
1962-1964

I drove directly from Cheyenne, Wyoming, to my new duty station in Bainbridge, MD. The all-female recruit training center for WAVEs located on the North-East bank of the Susquehanna River became my home from 1962 to 1964.

I looked and felt a bit of pain walking the three flights to my quarters. Even though the administration knew of my physical situation, they did not accommodate me. Walking those stairs drained my energy, but I did not complain. I did my duty, which was to coordinate the physical, first aid, and swimming training of these women recruited out of high school.

Even though I knew how to swim, and had never been close to drowning, I feared every time one of my less confident recruits practiced her strokes or floundered in the pool. I feared for the lives of the recruits who could not swim. For a year and a half, nightmares disturbed my sleep, so I enlisted the help of others who could swim. The nightmares continued. It seemed every night I drowned at least one of the young women looking to me for support.

During the last six months of my stay in Bainbridge, I became an assistant officer assigned to the commanding officer. I inspected the barracks, checked how the recruits made their beds, kept their lockers, cleaned the area, and how they wore their uniforms.

One day while walking to the barracks, I over-heard, "Here comes eagle eyes." I smiled, remembering these girls were still teenagers. I was molding them into women. Join the Navy and make a WAVE.

My duty remained as the head coordinator for the physical training in first aid classes. I completed the paperwork for each of my recruits. Keeping up with the mounds of required paper after a full day of teaching and supervising, became a tiring task. I had to check the documents of the entire company before each graduation. As each class graduated, I stood with the reviewing officers and felt proud.

When the bugle sounded "Taps" at the end of each day, I stood at attention in my office, saluted, then returned to the paperwork. It seemed my day never ended.

I smoked a couple of packs of Newport cigarettes every day. I started while a student at Denver University, and it

Captain Vail: Female Navy Trailblazer

Lt. Doris Vail (Official US Navy Photograph)

became a habit. After all, everybody smoked, why shouldn't I? I did not smoke in front of my recruits, or while on the grounds, but I lit up whenever I sat with the paperwork or needed a relaxing moment alone.

While stationed at Bainbridge, I had the opportunity to help our Under Secretary of the Navy, Paul B. Fay, a close friend of President Kennedy. On the day Mr. Fay was to review the graduating recruits, he asked me to watch over his children. The boy, Paul Fay, III, and his sister, Sally, and I talked and visited areas on the base. We sat together during the graduation ceremony, then toured the classrooms and the swimming pool. I felt happy to be asked to do this for Mr. Fay.

President Kennedy visited Bainbridge to open a major new highway. Kennedy was a young, handsome man, and our commander-in-chief. I watched his motorcade travel down HWY 40 and felt proud every time I saluted as his motorcade drove by.

I attended the Army/Navy game in 1963. As President Kennedy moved from the Navy side of the arena to the Army side at halftime, I stood close enough to his honor guard that I could have touched him. Instead, I stood at attention and saluted him.

I was working in my office on November 22, 1963, during President Kennedy's assassination. The entire company of 750 women broke down in mass hysteria. The recruits made so much noise, screaming and crying that the commanding

Captain Vail: Female Navy Trailblazer

Lt. Doris Vail with Under Secretary of the Navy children.
(Official US Navy Photograph)

officer told me to take the whole group somewhere to let them vent their feelings and get under control.

I marched them all to the movie theater. Unfortunately, the movie shown was PT 109 about President Kennedy as an ensign in the Navy during the Second World War. I asked the movie manager to show something else. He did. The recruits settled down. Task completed.

Life at Bainbridge was not only duty, teaching, and paperwork; there were also fun times. One of my enlisted handed me a rented Santa Claus suit, asked me to put it on and surprise the waiting company of recruits gathered for their Christmas party. I did. They ushered me into the gathering room. The surprise for the recruits, as we distributed gifts, brought the year to a successful close.

One of my honors at RTC was being the reviewing officer for the last class to graduate before I left for my next duty station in September 1964. I wrote my speech and presented it before the entire gathering sending all recruits to their first duty station.

*Lt. Doris Vail as Santa Claus.
(Official US Navy Photograph)*

6.
NAVSTA Rota, Spain
1964-1966

Naval Station Rota, also known as NAVSTA Rota, was and is a Spanish-American Naval Base commanded by a Spanish rear-admiral and funded by the United States of America. The base is the gate to the Mediterranean and includes an airfield and a port. It is close to the Straits of Gibraltar and is mid-distant between Southwest Asia and the United States of America.

With the rank of lieutenant and the only female assigned to the command, my job entailed an eight-hour day in the office assisting the commanding officer building a United States Security Station on a Spanish base. My time there passed quickly.

There were other female officers in Rota. They were teachers and nurses, but I served as the only female in the communication office. This created many obstacles. We solved the biggest—no designated lavatory for women.

The CO's office and mine were close together, so we shared the same lavatory. An embarrassing but funny incident happened when I walked in on him. The shock on his face and my blush caused us to laugh. But he did not forget to lock the door upon entering after that. He was a good guy but transferred before the end of my first year there.

At first, all the female officers—nurses, teachers, and me—lived in the BOQ, Bachelor Officer's Quarters, beside the men who partied all night. I moved into an apartment by myself in Juarez de la Frontera, about a 30-minute drive from base. Afterward, I rented a house on the beach in Rota.

Francisco Franco ruled Spain as a dictator. I often watched his soldiers armed with machine guns walk the streets. Franco's soldiers shot before asking questions, so orders circulated not to be on the beach after dark. Two of our Sailors partied on the beach after dark. Franco's men killed them.

The new CO, accompanied by his wife and children, arrived six months after me. He asked me to babysit his kids, which I was glad to do. I also babysat the son of one of my working buddies—a male officer. Babysitting came easily to me. I worked an eight-hour day, then relaxed on the beach or played golf. Often, I babysat for my commanding officer or another officer while they enjoyed Europe.

One child, a five-year-old, had leukemia. His mother asked me to help her with their son. Unexpectedly, the child died. I arranged the boy's memorial and his transport back to the United States. I felt glad to help the family but devastated the child was taken so soon.

Every afternoon, during our lunch break, the commander and a group of officers and I played golf. We had putting green contests won by the CO. I purchased my first set of golf clubs there, and my love for the game began.

As the recruiting poster notes, "Join the Navy and see the World," I refused to stay on base. I wanted to make the most of my time in Spain. I visited Portugal, London, The rock of Gibraltar, Casablanca, Barcelona, Madrid, Granada, and other spots in the area. Knowing I may not have this chance again, I took advantage of every minute during the two years stationed at Rota, Spain.

My sister, Donna, and her husband, Frank, visited. Frank became car sick and laid in the back seat because he couldn't handle the speed and narrow roads of Spain and Portugal. We stayed in an old, and I mean old, hotel. The beds were terrible, and the food a little scary.

After checking in, my sister headed for the lavatory down the hall. She locked herself in and banged on the door. By the time we heard her, it was late, and we were hungry.

"It's nine at night," she said, looking at the clock. "It's too late to eat. We can relax here in the room."

I said, "In Europe, the last meal doesn't start until nine at night. Let's go down."

We found no menu; the waiters served us the food of the day. They presented a considerable fish with skin and head intact. Donna's stomach screamed. She felt ill, so she put slices of lemon over the fish's eyes. "This way, the fish cannot watch me eat," she said.

The next day we drove across Spain to a friend of mine's home on a base where he was constructing a communication tower. My brother-in-law and I and my friend went to a bar for a drink or two or three. Donna stayed behind.

I said, "I'm not getting promoted. I think I may be passed-over this time." My next promotion would have been from lieutenant to lieutenant commander.

Frank lifted his glass of scotch. "Oh, no. You'll be promoted. They wouldn't dare pass you over."

I said, "It's difficult for a woman to be promoted. I'll bet you a case of scotch."

When I returned stateside, the Navy did promote me to lieutenant commander. I walked into a store in Maryland, saw a miniature set of scotch, bought it, and gave it to Frank. He blew up.

"You call this a case of scotch! You still owe me."

All these years, every time I see him, he talks about how I did not follow-up and do the right thing by sending him an actual "bona fide" case of scotch.

I ordered a custom-built Mercedes Benz from a factory in Frankfort, Germany, because I wanted to drive in style across Europe. My detailer called informing me I was needed in Washington DC and would receive orders to Naval Station Anacostia. I checked on my Mercedes, but the factory said it would not be complete until after my transfer.

Captain Vail: Female Navy Trailblazer

Mercedes like the one Doris Vail purchased in Spain.

Doris Vail

The night before I was due to leave Rota for my next duty station in the states, I visited one of the other officer's homes to say goodbye to his wife. The entire command arrived carrying cases of champagne. They threw a surprise farewell and thirtieth birthday party for me. We ate a huge dinner and drank throughout the evening. I spent the night at that officer's home in their guest room. When I woke the next morning, the empty champagne bottles lined the hall leading from my bedroom to the kitchen. After I hit the sack, my friends hit the halls, lining them with empty champagne bottles.

Unfortunately, or perhaps, fortunately, my flight was delayed and would not leave until 3 am., so we commenced partying again at my rented place.

By the time I arrived at the airport in New York City, all airlines had struck. I could not change planes to get to Cheyenne for three days, so I sat at the airport in uniform during those three days.

Then I heard, "All uniformed military personnel report to customer service." Standing in line with many military people waiting to board their flights brought relief and agitation. The airlines issued tickets on different small planes with frequent stops between New York and Wyoming. I arrived, but my suitcase did not.

After a day or so with my family in Cheyenne, the suitcase arrived. When unpacked, I discovered many champaign corks among my unmentionables. I remember Rota as a fun spot.

7.
Naval Station Anacostia
Washington DC
1966- 1969

I reported to Naval Station Anacostia in Washington DC, on August 11, 1966. I left Spain without my Mercedes, so I had to pay the customs into the United States, and other taxes that, if it had been ready on time when back in Europe, would not have been charged. But I wanted that Mercedes. I drove it for many years afterward.

The reason I liked this car so much was when I ordered it from the factory in Stuttgart, Germany, I paid $500 down, and they sent me samples of paint, inside material for seats and soft top of the convertible and examples for the hardtop. I got to have the car just like I wanted. I would then pick it up and drive it to the dock where the Navy would ship it to the US. This action would tag it as a used car limiting my taxes into the United States. My Navy detailer required me to transit back to the states before the factory completed the vehicle. This transfer reduced my time in Spain by two months.

Naval Station Anacostia served as a Naval support facility and headquarters for the chief of information. It contained a large heliport, used by Marine Helicopter Squadron One while supporting "Marine One" Presidential Transport operations. Admiral Zumwalt served as Chief of Naval Operations. He tasked me with setting up a family service center in the capitol.

The sixties was a decade of change and chaos. President Kennedy's assassination left Lyndon Johnson as United States President with an escalation to the war in Vietnam. Peace protests, the Anti-War Movement, the emergence of illegal drugs, and general unrest filled college campuses. The need for integration and peaceful changes to the racial laws led to riots. Military preparedness was a top priority, along with support for Naval families and personnel.

Promoted to lieutenant commander in 1968, I had free hand in setting up this first family center that became the forrunner to the present Fleet and Family Readiness Programs. My CO, a captain, supported my efforts by removing the occupying personnel from the office space I found and resourcing the area to me. I set about writing responsibilities for the office. I requested the personnel office responsible for writing all orders to copy those orders to me. Once that occurred, I lobbied private companies willing to provide bedding, towels, home starter sets, or dishes and cutlery for incoming Naval families.

This took every minute of my time working, but I enjoyed doing it. I designed and published pamphlets describing the items available and mailed them to families who had orders to DC. I maintained and stayed within the budget. As the families arrived, I became responsible for supplying those families with the items they needed. I completed all these tasks, unknowingly becoming a trailblazer.

The War in Vietnam continued. Women took the place of men stateside so the men could fight in Vietnam. The Navy refused to allow women into combat. Admiral Zumwalt changed the thinking of the role of women in the Navy. My role in this regard was to create the First Family Services Program. He charged me with another first. I created the First Transition Office, helping our Navy Servicemen returning from Vietnam find employment.

I coordinated with the US Labor Department and organized classes for these men in interview etiquette and resume writing. These we added to the newly formed Family Services Center.

This time in my service career was most rewarding because I had the freedom to create a service not done before. My staff and I helped many families and service members transition to the civilian world.

I found an apartment in Arlington, VA, just down the street from the Navy Annex. It was a one-bedroom on the

3rd floor of an enormous apartment building. I had a friend who lived in the building next to me. The back of the building was across the fence from the Army-Navy Golf Course.

While I had that apartment, my sister, Donna, and her husband Frank, came to see me with their two youngest children, twin boys, seven years old. They entertained everybody in the building because they got in the elevator and stayed there much too long. They loved riding up and down until we found them and got them out. I borrowed sleeping bags and fold- up beds so they could stay. Donna and Frank got my bed, and I slept on the couch. They went to the museums while I worked at Anacostia. After they left, two nieces stayed for about a week. I took them all over DC sightseeing.

We drove to Hershey, PA, and watched making chocolate. In those days, we walked through the factory and watched the making of chocolate up close. We also toured Williamsburg in Virginia. All my nieces and nephews came, two at a time, while I lived in that apartment.

On the day they assassinated Martin Luther King Junior, I stood as Officer on Duty. Rioters had taken control of much of Washington DC. Groups of rioters tried to enter Naval Base Anacostia, where the Presidential Boat, USS Sequoia, was harbored. We placed rolls of barbed wire fencing around the base. I carried a .45 ACP handgun as my sidearm.

I noticed a group of enlisted women on a bus trying to enter the base but being detained by an angry mob. The rioters attempted to push the bus over the bridge into the river. I jumped into a car and raced to the bus. I forced the rioters away from the bus so it could move on to the base. Then the women got into their barracks safely. It seemed like the world was on fire.

President Johnson dispatched 11,850 federal troops and 1,750 DC Army National Guardsmen to assist the police during these riots. The Army set up tents on the base tarmac directly in front of my office building. That was a terrible day. Thirteen people were killed in fires, by police officers, or by rioters. Statistics showed an additional 1,097 people injured, with over 7,600 people arrested.

Among all this, I decided it was time I return to a university to earn my Master of Science Degree in Personnel Administration. I attended night classes toward this goal. Orders to report to the Recruiting Headquarters in the Bureau of Naval Personnel came before I completed my degree.

8.
Washington DC
Bureau of Naval Personnel
Recruiting Headquarters Division
March 1969-1971
Bureau of Naval Personnel
—George Washington University
March 1971-1974
Bureau of Naval Personnel
March 1974-1976

I did not have to move when I transferred to the Recruiting Headquarters. I was closer to my duty station than when I was at Anacostia. After I started working at Recruiting Headquarters, I was working with a woman lieutenant commander who kept talking about not having a decent place to live. The two of us bought a house together in Vienna, VA, just eleven miles from the Navy Annex. The woman's name was Viola Curry.

I hurt my knee, so I had exploratory surgery at the Bethesda Naval Hospital. They placed a cast from hip to ankle. I missed three months of work because of the knee. Viola cared for me until she transferred to San Antonio, Texas.

Momma and Daddy came and stayed a month caring for me, my two cats, and two dogs. When they returned to Cheyenne, they began moving to Bullhead City in Arizona. I sat alone and watched all the bicentennial celebrations on television.

When I started using crutches, my boss picked me up each morning and returned me home after work every day. After the removal of the cast and some physical therapy, everything returned to normal. I purchased Viola's half of the house, so now I owned my first real estate.

I reported to the Bureau of Naval Personnel (BUPERS) in Washington DC on March 4, 1969, as a lieutenant commander. I reviewed every application from a woman wanting to join the Navy as an officer. There were enough applicants; we selected only the best for Officer Candidate School. I reviewed the high school and college transcripts and any information available about their leadership skills.

As part of my responsibility, I kept contact with naval college recruiters. The war in Vietnam and the anti-war demonstrations escalated, causing difficulties for our recruiters. Demonstrators spat upon our recruiters, rolled their cars over, and slashed tires. Morale plummeted, but the recruiters maintained control over themselves and continued doing their duty until the atmosphere became so uncomfortable, we removed the recruiters from college campuses. During all this confusion, I continued studying at night and received my Master of Science in personnel administration in the mail.

A Navy program selecting only ten officers a year for post graduate studies in a civilian university became available. My friends dared me to apply, so I did.

After being accepted at George Washington University to work on my Ph.D., I applied for the Navy program. I became the first female naval officer selected to study at a civilian school. Since then, more educational advances have become available to women in the Navy. I like to think I had a hand in that.

In January 1971, I received orders to report to George Washington University to begin my studies, while still being attached to the Bureau of Naval Personnel. I spent three years attending the university, working on my Ph.D.

On the first day of class, I wore my uniform, showing my rank as a lieutenant commander, but was spit upon while on campus. Anti-war fever ran rampant. Instead of directing the anger at the political establishment, the people directed it at anyone in a military uniform. The chief of naval operations put out a memo no longer requiring naval personnel in the DC area to wear uniforms. I spent a lot of my money purchasing appropriate business suits and heels. Although I did not hide, I was a military officer; I wore civilian clothing to class. The locals no longer spit upon me. How could people I swore to protect be so disrespectful? The United States pulled out of Vietnam, and the POWs arrived home in 1973.

Before completing my dissertation, I received orders to return to the Bureau of Naval Personnel as head of the Officer Strength Planning section. Before reporting for duty, I decided I would better serve at ICAF, the Industrial College of the Armed Forces, at Ft. McNair in Washington DC.

Created in 1943, The Army Industrial College taught military contracting officers how to end contracts without bankrupting companies. In 1945, the name of the school changed to The Industrial College of the Armed Forces or ICAF. Thinking I could finish my dissertation while working there, I requested an interview with the CO.

He, an army colonel, listened patiently, then shook his head, "You've never heard the sound of a gun on the battlefield. The students have. I don't think they will accept you. Besides, no woman has taught at this institution." He dismissed me. I returned to my position as the officer in charge of the Strength Plans Section at the Bureau of Naval Personnel.

In 1974, discussions began changing the restrictions placed upon female naval personnel. Admiral Zumwalt, the nineteenth Chief of Naval Operations (1970-1974), had written directives called Z-Grams revising, modernizing, and equalizing opportunities for Women In the Navy. Among other ideas, Z-116 opened ratings to enlisted women, established a pathway for assigning women to ships, and opened all staff corps and restricted line communities to women.

Whenever the opportunity arrived to speak about Women In the Navy, I lobbied hard for change. When I joined the WAVEs back in 1958, only five percent of the entire naval force was female. Twenty years later, ten percent of the force was female. Restrictions on female recruitment, promotion, career choice, educational opportunity, and social life contributed to the attrition rate. A social and cultural change occurred during the sixties and seventies. More women enlisted. The ban on marriage and childbearing lifted. Women proved they could excel in non-traditional jobs. The drafting of men ended, creating a greater need for both male and female enlistments.

I got busy right away developing rules for all the Navy on how to accommodate women in various jobs and to ensure fair treatment for them in non-traditional roles. I changed the focus of my dissertation to assessing the leadership of the groups of women in their non-traditional roles. I again requested an interview with the new CO of ICAF.

9.
Industrial College of the Armed Forces
ICAF

I requested an interview with the new CO of ICAF. He recommended the Navy provide orders for me to become the first female instructor at the Industrial College of the Armed Forces. I reported there in September 1976 with the rank of commander.

The new CO assisted me in my goal toward a Ph.D. by assigning a senior male officer as my travel companion to help with conducting interviews in an effort they would remain unbiased. We each interviewed and recorded one hundred enlisted men and women. We identified the differences in the leadership of groups of men and women working together in a traditional workgroup vs. a group with women working together in non-traditional jobs alongside men. The CO supplied computer time to assess the statistics proving my thesis, which I defended in October 1978.

I taught personnel administration, labor-management relations, organizational behavior, and organizational change as the first female instructor at ICAF.

Even though I had not "heard the sound of gunfire during war," my students accepted me. I had something of interest to teach them and knew my material. Released POWs from Vietnam attended this school, as did other higher-ranking officers. Military policy stated released soldiers, Sailors, and airmen from the service may need help to acclimate to civilian life during peacetime. Although three years had passed since the release of the last known POW's from Vietnam, the government assigned them as students at ICAF.

Meeting these ex-POWs became the highlight of my life. They had been tortured in prison and isolated for five years. They told us about how they communicated with each other through the walls. They memorized the Bible and some poetry to help them cope. It was a pleasure having these students. Their sense of humor and appreciation for everything gave me a feeling of awe.

Students who had not undergone the same situations complained about everything—assigned homework, schedule of classes, student expectations. The ex-POWs complained about nothing. As the only woman on the faculty, I enjoyed being an instructor at ICAF and made many lasting friendships. During my last year at ICAF, I met a woman student with the same rank as mine. It was a pleasure having her as my student.

A blizzard blew into the area the day 9 February 1979, I was to graduate with my long-awaited Ph.D. in business administration. The deep snow made it impossible to drive. The blizzard canceled graduation; my cap, hood, gown and diploma arrived in the mail. I felt disappointed not to receive this degree on stage, but life goes on.

Many changes occurred for Women In the Navy during the time I was at ICAF. Ongoing discussions about assigning women to ship duty required different accommodations. Congress changed the law providing women the right to be promoted to captain and then admiral and releasing the restriction on the number of women needed. The Navy lifted restrictions on marriage, and childbearing necessitating new maternity uniforms. In a surprise move, the Navy promoted me to captain.

10.
Enlisted Strength Plans Division
1980-1982

The eighties ushered in a decade of relative peace. The Cold War between The United Soviet Socialist Republic or the communist countries and the United States or free democratic countries threatened nuclear annihilation. Wars continued in the Middle East and South America. The American economy boomed, and defense spending raised. The space program progressed, racial integration and the war on drugs continued.

Jimmy Carter became US President after Nixon resigned, then Ronald Reagan beat Carter in the election of 1980. The Reagan Era of relative peace and prosperity began.

In May 1980, my orders changed to Enlisted Strength Plans Division still in Washington, DC. I met Helen there. We developed a lifelong friendship. Helen became an Automatic Data Processor (ADP). She did so well in that field she ended up being the division head of all Navy classified communications.

Later, in 2011, she replaced communications destroyed in the Pentagon on 9/11. She was awarded the highest civil service award for her accomplishments.

We became roommates in 1980 and maintained our companionship for forty years.

As a captain, I had responsibility for the planning of the recruitment of people in every naval occupation. I analyzed numbers, filled all billets with qualified individuals, and supervised a workforce of both men and women.

In my spare time, I played golf.

Captain Vail: Female Navy Trailblazer

The Pentagon on September 11, 2001
(US Navy Photography)

11.
Deputy Director of Personnel Plans Programming and Budgeting
OP-12
1982-1984

In July 1982, the Navy assigned me as the Deputy Director of Personnel Plans Programming and Budgeting or OP-12. After 25 years serving my country, I held the rank of captain—just one rating below admiral.

One-hundred people worked for me. My CO was a male two-star admiral, close to retirement. He was away for one month, so I became the acting director. A memo circulated informing me of a meeting the director was to attend, so I did.

I took a seat at the front of the table, close to the briefer's podium. A voice boomed: "Captain Vail. What are you doing here? This meeting is for admirals only."

I stood, looked at the boomer, a captain just like me, and said, "I am acting Director of Personnel Plans Program and Budgeting. I am required to attend this meeting." Every admiral seated nodded his head, showing they agreed with me. I sat.

During the briefing, I contributed when required, and everyone accepted me as their equal.

Often, I held meetings in my office for every branch head who worked under me. These meetings were informal, but I noticed after a few months, fewer heads attended. I asked my secretary why they didn't seem to want to meet in my office.

"They do not like the smoke," she said.

It was May 13th. I remember the date because I quit smoking cold turkey and never regretted it. I started smoking while attending Denver University and had worked my way up to four packs a day. It's a wonder I didn't have lung cancer or emphysema.

I worked all day in my office, keeping track of programs In the Navy, and of their budgets. I wrote papers, attended congressional meetings, and lobbied for a change in the regulations. During after hours, I enjoyed listening to music, spending time with friends, and a good game of golf.

As a visiting professor for George Mason University in Fairfax, I taught organizational behavior and change in the MBA program. All my classes were at night or on weekends. I worked ten to twelve hours every day, plus prepared and taught college classes. The substantial stress of working as

Captain Vail: Female Navy Trailblazer

Capt. Doris Vail Retires.
(US Navy Photograph)

deputy director of OP-12 contributed to the absolute fatigue I felt.

An admiral friend of mine suggested I go to San Diego for an interview as the Head of the Navy Personnel Research and Development Agency. The station demanded an admiral's rating. Regulations permitted the promotion of only one female captain to one-star admiral. I considered my options but felt exhausted and needed rest. I retired.

12.
Captain Doris Vail Retires
August 1, 1984

On August 1, 1984, after 26 years of Naval service, Captain Doris Vail retired. Vice Admiral Lawrence, Chief of Naval Personnel, presented her with her second Navy Legion of Merit Award and Medal for outstanding service while serving as deputy director of the total force programming and manpower division of CNP from July 1982 through August 1984.

Vice Adm. Lawrence said, "She has demonstrated superior performance in all phases of her duties, displaying a comprehensive knowledge of Navy manpower, personnel, and training. The positive impact she had on this arena was of incalculable value to the Navy and will be felt for many years."

As I listened to the speeches from many of the people I

worked with over the years, my eyes clouded, realizing the impact I had on both the individuals I worked with and the programs I created. One of my friends who had been a Prisoner of War in Vietnam and who I taught at ICAF presented me with a certificate.

My family attended. My father, who had not wanted me to join, stood firm and so proud he nearly busted out of his suit. I smiled, remembering the times he had visited during my career and realized how vital serving was to me. I felt honored to have served my country for twenty-six years. I like to think because of my actions, women today have more opportunities for advancement in the Navy. Join the Navy; it is an enjoyable and rewarding life.

Capt. Doris Vail at retirement party.

Captain Vail: Female Navy Trailblazer

*Retirement Ceremony.
Doris' family is in the front row.
(US Navy Photograph)*

Doris Vail

(L-R) Donald Vail, Capt. Doris Vail, Dorothy Vail.
(US Navy Photograph)

Captain Vail: Female Navy Trailblazer

Captain Doris Vail with family. (L-R) Brother-in-law Frank Hellwig, Sister Donna Hellwig, Capt. Vail, Mother Dorothy Vail, Father Donald Vail. (US Navy Photograph)

13.
Vail retires from Navy

Captain Doris Ruth Vail, USN, daughter of Mr. and Mrs. Donald Vail of Riveria Arizona, formerly of Cheyenne, Wyoming, was recently presented her second Navy Legion of Merit during Washington D.C. retirement ceremonies.

She was honored by naval officials and coworkers at the Office of the Deputy Chief of Naval Operations for Manpower Personnel and Training/Chief of Naval Personnel (CNP) for 26 outstanding years of naval services.

Vice Admiral William P Lawrence presented the award to Vail for exceptionally meritorious conduct in the performance of outstanding service "while serving as deputy director of the total force programming and manpower division of CNP from July 1982 through August 1984.

She was cited for "demonstrating superior performance in all phases of her duties, (which) displayed unparalleled comprehensive knowledge of Navy manpower, personnel, and training.

The positive impact she had on this arena was of incalculable value to the Navy and will be felt for many years.

She received a Bachelor of Arts degree in special education from the University of Denver, Colorado., in 1958 and was commissioned an ensign in August of that year. She first reported for duty at Naval Communications Station, San Diego, CA.

In July 1960, Lieutenant junior grade Vail transferred to Naval Air Station North Island, California. She reported for her first East Coast assignment in May 1962 at the Recruit Training Command in Bainbridge, Maryland.

Then Lieutenant Vail transferred to Naval Communication Station in Rota, Spain. In October 1964, she returned stateside and in August 1966 reported to the Naval Station in Washington DC, where she was an official officer in charge of establishing the Navy's first family service center. She was also responsible for several other "quality of life" program firsts while assigned to Washington Naval Station, Anacostia.

In March 1969, Lieutenant Commander Vail transferred to the Bureau of Naval Personnel in Washington DC. During this assignment, she received a Master of Arts degree in personal administration from George Washington University in Washington, DC.

She was selected for the direct enrollment doctoral

program at George Washington University in January 1971 and returned to the Bureau of Naval Personnel in March 1974.

Commander Vail became an instructor at the Industrial College of the Armed Forces in August 1976 and received her doctorate in business administration from George Washington University in 1979.

Captain Vail first reported to CNP in May 1980 as head of the enlisted programs implementations branch of the military personnel policy division.

She became deputy director of the total force programming and manpower division in July 1982. In this position, she assisted the director in ensuring the proper mix of manpower, material, and fiscal resources needed to meet worldwide Naval objectives.

Among her other awards and decorations are the Defense Meritorious Service Medal and the National Defense Service Medal.

Vail will remain in northern Virginia following her retirement; She resides in Vienna, Va.

14.
After The Navy

Not quite old enough to retire to a rocking chair and whittle my life away, but tired of the daily grind, I stayed connected to the Navy through newspapers and talking to friends on active duty.

In 1985, I applied and taught undergraduates at George Mason University in Fairfax, Virginia. Teaching gave me a different view of my life, so after the first year teaching day classes, I switched back to teaching in the MBA program where most of the students worked during the daytime and took classes at night and on weekends. After three years of teaching, I needed to do other things.

I attended Real Estate School, got my license, and purchased a house with my friend, Helen. She and I had maintained our friendship while she worked at the Navy Annex. Upon graduation from Real Estate School, I worked

Doris Vail

for a small company in McLean, Virginia, starting as the manager of 25 properties. Six years later, when I quit the company, I had become responsible for 250 properties, including companies located in the antique area of Fairfax, Virginia.

I stopped working and played golf every day at Ft. Belvoir, an Army post in Springfield, Virginia. They elected me president of the group, then chairman of the local tournament. Being in charge came naturally to me; I knew how to delegate. I became tired with so much work, playing golf, and general living and health concerns.

15.
The Ranch

In 1946, when I was eleven years old, my parents purchased a 223-acre ranch in the mountains, more than a three-hour drive from Cheyenne. The Colorado/Wyoming state line ran right through our property, so we paid taxes in both states. The family, including aunts, uncles, and cousins, often gathered on the ranch. I spent many summers during my early years working on the farm with my grandfather.

I recall Grandpa Jake had a long barrel gun in the cabin. Whenever we spied a rodent skittering by, he'd say, "Shoot 'um," and I shot the varmint.

In 1986, just two years after I retired, the entire clan, including 27 family members, gathered for our 40th-year celebration. We set up tents around the house, and people slept in sleeping bags.

My brother, Dexter, drove his recreational vehicle, so his

family did not sleep on the ground. Daddy and I cooked a large breakfast of pancakes, bacon, eggs, and coffee on the wood-burning stove. Twenty-seven of us ate together, talking and laughing.

(L-R) Doris, Donna, Dorothy, Donald, Dexter at the Ranch 40th Anniversary 1986.

Captain Vail: Female Navy Trailblazer

*The Ranch.
(Painting by R. Chinery)*

16.
International Women Veterans Golf Association

In 1988 I joined the International Women veterans Golf Association (IWVGA). A group of discharged military women started the IWVGA, known as the ruptured ducks, in 1976. The membership was and is open to all women veterans. The association sponsored a three-day golf tournament somewhere every year. I played in the competition for several years.

According to association rules, several guests may accompany each contestant. For seventeen years, my brother, Dexter, competed as my guest. Everyone enjoyed having him, and he enjoyed traveling with the ladies to the many places at which we held competitions. In 2000, Dexter's wife, Ilene, and my sister, Donna, accompanied us to El Cajon, California. Neither Ilene nor Donna played, but they enjoyed the camaraderie and family companionship.

We members always have a wonderful time flying together and competing in unique places where we explored new settings. Any veteran female golfer, regardless of handicap, could join this group. At the start, a WAVE from the British Navy on assignment in the United States took part. After she left, another from Canada on an exchange program in the United States joined the group, making it an international golf organization. As of this writing, 2020, I contribute to this group and enjoy golf.

Tournaments Where and When

Myrtle Beach, South Carolina	1988
Lake Havasu, Arizona	1989
Air Force Academy, Colorado	1992
Las Cruces, New Mexico	1993
Fort Lewis, Tacoma, Washington	1994
Fort Sam Houston, Texas	1995
Reno, Nevada	1996
Biloxi, Mississippi	1998
Fort Huachuca, Arizona	1999
El Cajon, California	2000
Redmond, Oregon	2001
Andrews Air Force Base, Maryland	2002
Las Vegas, Nevada	2003
Maui, Hawaii	2004
Hilton Head, South Carolina	2005
Rohnert Park, California	2006

Wild Dunes, South Carolina	2007
Reno, Nevada	2008
Golf Hall of Fame, Florida	2009
Ft Sam Houston, Texas	2010
San Antonio, Texas	2011
Klamath Falls, Oregon	2012
Mayport Naval Station, Florida	2014
Admiral Baker Golf Course, San Diego, CA.	2015
Mobile, Alabama	2016
Reno, Nevada	2017
Sequim, Washington	2018
Tunica, Mississippi	2019

17.
The Women's Memorial

Of the 214 monuments and memorials in Washington DC, the Women In Military Service for America Memorial or WIMSA is housed inside the Hemicycle that serves as the entrance to Arlington Cemetery. On June 23, 1995, I joined many women in and out of uniform, who served in time of war or peace as Army WACs, Navy WAVEs, in the Air Force or the National Guard or Coast Guard. Many came in wheelchairs and with canes.

Retired Air Force Brig. Gen. Wilma L. Vaught, who served in Vietnam, took charge of the ceremony as she had held the reins on building support for the memorial. Huge tents held space for women from each service in the crowd for this groundbreaking ceremony.

I joined a group of Navy women for lunch on the lawn of the National Mall, before walking to the ceremony in front of

Doris Vail

Arlington Cemetery, where I became one of the first female veterans to register at the Woman's Memorial. I am called a plank owner of the memorial. That evening, I thought about my time in the service and how my work made a difference for women in the Navy today.

Captain Vail: Female Navy Trailblazer

The Women's Memorial at Arlington National Cemetery.

18.
Personal Life

Life after the military was not all fun and games. In 1999, the doctor informed me I had breast cancer. After surgery and five weeks of radiation therapy, I felt well enough to continue my favorite pastime—playing golf.

To ease some of the stress, Helen and I purchased a cabin in West Virginia next to the golf course of Cacapon State Park. We drove up there every weekend to play golf.

Helen and I built another house just for the experience. We used our money and my realtor expertise to build a home in Fredericksburg, Virginia. We had become owners of three houses.

In the meantime, Helen's parents had become ill, so we drove from Virginia to Melbourne, Florida, where they lived. In 2006, Helen and I moved closer to her parents. Our new home, in Green Cove Springs, Florida, caused only a three-hour drive to help with her parents in Melbourne. After Helen's father passed away, her mother lived with us in Green Cove.

After Helen's mother died, we left our home in Green Cove Springs and moved north to Rehoboth Beach in Delaware. We joined our friends in Delaware in 2013, but after three years of shoveling snow and freezing, we returned to Florida.

In 2016, we purchased our present home in The Villages, Florida.

19.
Momma and Daddy

No one paid much attention to family history; we were too busy living, so what I know about the two sides of my family is a bit sketchy. Like all Americans, the original Vail family came from somewhere else. To top that off, the Vail family adopted my father's grandfather, so I have no record of his family's history.

Earl Vail, my grandfather, married my grandmother, Madge, probably in Decker, Michigan, sometime in the early 1900s. Earl and Madge had two children, my father, Donald, born September 19, 1907, in Decker, Michigan, and his sister, Ruth. Madge and Earl divorced. Earl traveled to California, where he married Gertrude.

Dad was fifteen years old when Madge married Earl's brother, Rowland. I grew up calling my grandfather, Rowland Vail, Uncle Rollie, since he was my father's uncle. Madge and

Uncle Rollie moved from Decker to Flint, Michigan.

As a teenager, Donald hitch-hiked from Michigan to California to be with his father, Earl Vail. He and his stepmother didn't get along, so Donald hitched back to Michigan through Nebraska, where he worked on the farms, one of which belonged to Jacob Carey.

Daddy met Momma. Momma, born Dorothy Mae Carey, on September 14, 1910, lived on a farm with her sister, brother, and father, Jacob, called Jake.

The Carey family migrated to the United States from England. Grandpa Jake told me he remembered traveling by covered wagon probably over the Oregon Trail from Iowa to Nebraska when he was seven years old. "I walked mostly," he said, "the wagon was full of my family and our stuff."

Grandpa Jake became a farmer in Hebron, Nebraska, where he married Laura Heffner, whose family hailed from Germany. Laura died of asthma when Momma was nine years old. Momma, born September 14, 1910, in Hebron raised her little sister, Wilma. She completed high school and teacher training becoming a teacher in the one-room schoolhouse in Hebron.

While Daddy and Momma courted, Grandpa Jake met with my father outside the farm and told him to leave Momma alone and go away. Daddy did. He continued to Flint, Michigan, but wrote love letters back to my mother.

Momma followed him. They married in Flint, Michigan, on October 4, 1928. A year later, on December 22, 1929,

Momma gave birth to my brother, Dexter, and on May 24, 1933, to my sister, Donna. Daddy worked at a filling station until the Great Depression hit them hard. Dad could no longer sustain his family on fifty cents an hour.

Dad, Momma, Dexter, and Donna loaded into their 1930 Ford Model A automobile and drove toward Colorado, where Grandpa Jake lived. With only fifteen dollars in his pocket, Daddy relied on the friendly feelings of local farmers who took them in and helped when their automobile broke down. As they drove to Loveland, Colorado, where Momma's father lived with a friend, the car chugging up a hill, quit. They abandoned it on the side of the road.

Momma and Daddy set up a house in a trailer on the same plot as Grandpa Jake lived. Daddy worked for the highway department laying gravel on roads in the area. I was born on October 21, 1935, in Colorado. Six weeks later, our family moved to Cheyenne, Wyoming.

Momma's brother, Byrle, owned a farm in Cheyenne, so Grandpa Jake moved in with him and his family. Grandpa Jake's sister, Mate, owned a grocery store, so Momma and Daddy bought a house across the street. Dad worked in a creamery in Cheyenne and spent three years washing milk bottles. He then worked as a switchman on the Union Pacific Railroad in Cheyenne for thirty-three years. The work was strenuous. Before unionization, he worked seven days a week with no time off. He saved as much money as possible.

When Momma's brother, Byrle, divorced his wife, who

lived down the street from us, Momma raised their son, my cousin, Bill, who was six weeks older than me. Both Bill and I became adventure seekers. He and I often ran around the area looking to discover exciting places. Since our older siblings attended public school, we often dropped into their classrooms for a visit. Their teacher told us to return home.

One day Bill and I crossed over the viaduct into downtown Cheyenne where we found a candy store. We promised our Mom would pay for an all-day sucker, so the clerk gave one to each of us. We headed back home but stopped to rest with our little legs stuck between the rails of the viaduct watching the men build the bus station.

Mom drove by, saw us, and turned around. We got into her car, and she returned Bill to his mother's home, then took me to mine, where she sent me to bed after relinquishing my sucker to my sister, Donna. I never ran away again.

While stationed at Anacostia Naval Base in 1968, Momma and Daddy moved into a double-wide trailer home in Bullhead City, Arizona, next door to Uncle Byrle. Daddy and Uncle Byrle often fished from their boat or sailed across the river into Riviera Nevada, where they gambled.

Momma became sick. She had cancer. Dexter, who lived in Montana, Donna, lived in Denver, Colorado, and I, who lived in Vienna, Virginia, shared helping them in Arizona. We decided Momma and Daddy needed to move in with one of us. They bought a home in Montana. Dexter drove by their place every day on his way to work.

After a few months of chemotherapy for her lung cancer, Momma forwent therapy and passed away on March 12, 1994. Daddy took turns living with each of us kids. He spent three months with Donna in Colorado, three months with me in Virginia, and six months with Dexter in Montana. Six years later, he got sick while living with Dexter. He wanted to see the new year 2000, so Donna and I visited with him at Dexter's place. We watched television as the ball came down, and the New year swept across the world. He passed on January 19, 2000.

Doris and Cousin Bill ready to set off on one of their adventures.

Doris Vail

20.
Family Serving America

Even though I traveled extensively and did not live close to family, I remained in contact with them through the years. One of the most surprising calls from the family came in 2016, when my great-nephew, Karl Hellwig, asked me to not only attend his commissioning ceremony at the Air Force Academy in Colorado Springs but to administer the oath to him. Karl finished his four years at the Academy. I felt honored to commission him into officer status in the Air Force.

Karl continued his studies at dental school and after four years in tact school in Denver, he graduated and received orders to Omaha, Nebraska as an air force dentist.

Doris Vail

Retired Cpt. Doris Vail   2nd Lt. Karl Hellwig

Retired Capt. Doris Vail, Kurt Hellwig (Karl's father), 2nd Lt. Karl Hellwig, Michelle Hellwig (Karl's step-mother).

Donna and Doris on the ferry to Oxford, MD during their annual bike trip, May 1993.

Doris, Donna and Helen take a lunch break on a bike trip near Nokesville, VA in September, 2003

21.
Yearly Bicycle Rides

My sister, Donna, and I planned trips on our bicycles across the country to various spots of interest. On April 16, 1996, Donna flew from Denver, Colorado to Vienna, Virginia, for our first bicycle adventure. We stowed our bikes on the bike rack at the rear of my car and headed out to Nags Head, North Carolina. The following day, we rode our bicycles from the motel in Kitty Hawk to the Wright Brothers Museum. After the eighteen-mile ride fighting wind and sand, we felt tired. Is it worth continuing? You bet it is.

The next day, we loaded our bikes and drove to Hatteras, where we caught the ferry across to Ocracoke Island. We parked the car and rode our bikes 14.5 miles into town and back. What a lovely ride, the scenery breathtaking, and the history absorbing, not to mention the food. Upon our return, we were the last car on the ferry.

The third day of this trip took us to the lost colony of Roanoke Island. In 1587, John White and 115 others colonized the area. The first child born in the New World, Virginia Dare, was buried there. When White returned three years after leaving, he found no trace of its inhabitants, other than a few clues to what might have happened apart from a single word—"Croatoan"—carved into a wooden post.

We returned to Vienna, Virginia, and took the Metro downtown to the Holocaust Museum and The Korean War Memorial. History has always been an interest of mine, so whenever I have the chance and the means, I explore.

From September 16-26, 1997, while Dad stayed with me in Virginia, we celebrated his ninetieth birthday. Donna and Dexter visited. The five of us, Dad, Donna, Dexter, Helen, and I drove to our house in Lake of the Woods in Locust Grove, Virginia. Helen and I built that home as a weekend release from our work. We spent our weekends there, playing golf and fishing. Helen's mother and father from Florida have temporarily lived in our house

After a brief visit to Locust Grove, we returned to Vienna, so Dexter and Daddy could fly back to Kalispell, Montana. Donna and I drove with our bicycles loaded to Cape Cod, Massachusetts. We rode all over the Cape. We got lost and had to call the motel for help.

The next day, we rode our bicycles and caught the ferry to Martha's Vineyard. All along the line, we sampled grape wine and fabulous foods. Donna left for Denver on September 26, leaving Helen and me to carry on.

From October 8-14, 1998, Donna visited me in Virginia. We attended the National Symphony Concert at the Kennedy Center, then packed our bikes and drove up to the cabin by Berkeley Springs, West Virginia. On the tenth, we biked ten miles over the mountain to Berkeley Springs for the Apple Butter Festival. A large kettle containing apple cider boiled over a fire on the street in the center of town. We purchased several jars of apple butter after watching the people fill the jars from that kettle. We placed the heavy jars on our bike handlebars, which made our ten-mile return trip over the mountain to our cabin, slow.

I noticed a pickup truck with a rifle hung behind the driver, following us. We became concerned, so we pulled off the road and stopped, hoping the driver would pass us. He did. I breathed a silent prayer of thanks.

The following morning we packed up the bikes and apple butter before driving to our house at Lake of the Woods by Fredericksburg, Virginia. We toured the Civil War battlefields, then returned to our home and rested enjoying each other's company. Donna left Vienna by plane, returning to Denver.

From October 19-27, 2000, Donna visited me for my sixty-fifth birthday. We loaded our bicycles once again and drove up to the cabin. We drove to Harper's Ferry, carried our bikes over the bridge, and down two flights of stairs. Imagine two older women lugging bicycles and then riding thirty miles along the path by the Chesapeake and Ohio Canal. We then traveled twelve miles to Shepherds Town bridge and back. Riders on horses, other bikers, and hikers waved and smiled. The warmth of the day, our enjoyment at being together, taking in the beautiful countryside filled my heart with joy.

We got the bikes back up the flights of stairs and back to the car in the parking lot. We had ridden them from 12:30 to 5:00 pm before driving back to the cabin. We felt tired and exhilarated.

On the next day, we drove the car to a big pool parking lot, unloaded our bikes and traveled on an old paved train bed. We rode seventeen miles and stopped at Frederick State Park. We had no ticket, so we looked through the slats on the fence. We saw the old barracks and parade ground restored in 1974. We returned to Vienna the next day.

While at home, we visited all the Smithsonian museums, shopped a bit, and attended concerts at the Kennedy Center. Donna returned to Denver on the twenty-seventh. What a lovely time we had together. It wasn't our last.

I made reservations at a bed-and-breakfast motel on Tangier Island, Maryland, an island in the center of the Chesapeake Bay for Donna's visit on September 29, 2001. We parked behind the hardware store, spent the night at the Paddle Wheel Motel, and packed our backpacks for a one-night stay, and rode our bikes to the ferry for the trip to Tangier Island. The voyage was rough, as the seas were high and the air cold. We made reservations to take the return trip to Chrisfield the next day, but the ferry canceled the trip because a storm hit the water. Not deterred, we spent that day riding our bikes around the small island with a population of 720.

We watched a talent show at the local high school, attended church, and enjoyed conversations with the local people. People spoke with an accent reminiscent of old English mixed with modern English. A coffin set in front of every house. For years, ocean waves and hurricanes hit this island, causing the loss of landmass and the unearthing of graves. It was not unusual to find pieces of caskets or bones washed ashore.

With the ferry closed, because of a winter storm, the motel owner arranged a trip back to Chrisfield for us on a small mail boat. The boatman, named Larry, agreed to take us to Smith Island for the night. The proprietor at the B&B at Smith Island waited for us. The boat we took was small, the water rough, the weather terrible, we feared we would overturn. Instead, we became soaked as the water came through the windows. This is another time I knew God watched over us and saved our lives.

We left our bikes and backpacks on the boat at Smith Island and walked to the Bed and Breakfast. The proprietor and his wife were retired history professors.

With no dry clothing in which to sleep, and none to wear in the morning, and the wind howling outside, we had a tough night sleeping.

We returned to the boat. The boatman took us back to Crisfield, where we found our car and loaded our bikes on the bike rack. By this time, the winter storm had turned to snow. We drove back to Vienna and spent the evening washing clothes and trying to get warm. I thanked the Lord, once again, for getting us home in one piece.

Donna visited Vienna again in 2002 and 2003, bringing her bike each time. We enjoyed biking, sightseeing, and attending concerts and museums. I know she enjoyed these times as much as I did. As sisters, we had a good relationship and shared many wonderful memories.

Doris and Donna at lunch on top of a mountain.

22.
Fort Lauderdale Airport Shooting
January 6, 2017

My roommate, Helen, and I planned an eleven-day cruise through the Panama Canal with a visit to Costa Rica in January 2017. Our friend Kathy agreed to join us. The weather in Florida was cool, but we were going closer to the equator, so it didn't bother us. We did, however, take our jackets.

Helen's sister, Laura, lived in Coral Springs close to Fort Lauderdale, where we were to catch our flight to Panama and begin our vacation. We drove from The Villages to Coral Springs and left our car at Laura's house. Kathy joined us there. Before Laura drove us to the airport, I placed my medicines in the required zip lock baggies, checked we had our passports, and money and my prescription sunglasses.

Once inside the terminal, we stood in line and proceeded through security.

I passed through the gate first and waited in front of Helen while she placed her shoes in the bin. Before picking up my bags, purse and passport from the bin, I heard "pow, pow."

Something was going on. The Transportation Security Agents looked up from their jobs, saying, "Run. Everybody leave the building. Now." All around I heard people running from the airplane gates toward me, their faces filled with fear.

Chaos seemed to engulf the area. People turned, grabbed their children, bumping into each other, trying to get as far away from where we were as quickly as possible. Helen bent down to pick up her bags but had to leave her shoes. I grabbed my backpack, overnight bag, and purse, but someone bumped into me so hard, I lost my balance. My bags flew through the air in different directions. I landed on the floor and lost track of both Helen and Kathy.

"What are you doing down there?" A uniformed TSA agent asked. He pulled me up. "Stay close. Follow me."

We ran through the halls in a mass of people. Helen, Where's Helen? I stepped inside an open door to one shop along the corridor, looking at the people, hoping to see Helen.

"Helen, over here." I beckoned. She joined me. She wore no shoes and had no purse or bag.

We passed through a bar on the way to the tarmac. Broken glass scattered on the floor, tables overturned, people sprawled on and under the tables. A woman in an overturned wheelchair yelled for help. We stopped, but the horde pushed us further. We arrived outside; people pushed their way down the stairs. A woman carrying a basket and pushing a baby in a stroller while holding onto a toddler tried to move down the steps. Helen took the stroller, and I the toddler's hand. We helped them down.

Police officers gathered the crowd onto the tarmac, directing us into safe zones. No one knew what was happening. Was there a bomb? Is this a terrorist attack? Where is Kathy?

We stood or sat on the cold concrete with no food, no water, no cellphone, no information. Helen walked over the glass in her bare feet, so they were cut up. We found no first aide. A woman offered her cellphone.

"Do you know your sister's phone number?" she asked Helen.

"I can't think," Helen said.

"Where does she live?"

We told the lady who called the police station in Coral Springs.

Meanwhile, we waited. Still no sign of Kathy.

After dark, the police opened the terminal and ushered us in a closed line through the center of the area. The FBI had finished searching. There had been a mass shooting claiming five deaths, six wounded, and thirty-five injuries. In the aftermath, TSA agents distributed forms to file claims. We could not look for our luggage; the airport personnel had collected it and put it in a warehouse.

Kathy walked up to us. "I've been behind a counter in a store. The police found us and told us to stay put until they released us. I am fine. They said the gunfire might have come from an agent at the gate."

I noticed a man changing his son, who was soaking wet, but he had nothing for the boy to wear, and it was getting cold. Helen noticed a stack of unused plastic bags. We distributed the bags to the parents and families around us so they could use them to protect against the chill.

An agent circulated, showing people photos he had taken of the possessions he had collected. I saw my coat, so he retrieved it, but not my medicine, purse, luggage, or passport. Lunch areas and drink stands closed, so we could find nothing to eat or drink. I saw the workers ordered pizza, but they walked past us and took it into a back room.

We slept on the floor that night. In the morning, Helen's sister, Laura, arrived and drove us back to her house where we stayed for six days.

Helen and I returned to The Villages after 6 days during which we got some of our belongings brought to us at Laura's house. A FEDX truck delivered the rest of our belongings to us at The Villages. My prescription sunglasses never showed up.

After haggling with the insurance agency, we received a check only for the price of the cruise, not for the six days of medicine I had to purchase, or my prescription sunglasses.

Captain Vail: Female Navy Trailblazer

*Kathy, Helen and Doris
during the ordeal at Ft. Lauderdale Airport.*

The police had not called this situation terror-related.

Terror related? Absolutely. I still see the fear on the people's faces who knocked me down, nearly trampling me. I still feel the fear of losing my friend, Helen, and the panic surrounding us.

A mass shooting occurred at Fort Lauderdale–Hollywood International Airport in Broward County, Florida, United States, on January 6, 2017, near the baggage claim in Terminal 2. Five people were killed while six others were injured in the shooting. About 36 people sustained injuries in the ensuing panic.

> Date: January 6, 2017
> Number of deaths: 5
> Location: Fort Lauderdale-Hollywood International Airport, FL
> Injured: ± 42 (6 gunshot victims, around 36 with other injuries)
> Attack type: Mass shooting
> Weapons: Walther PPS 9mm semi-automatic pistol

23.
Villages Life

Helen and I moved into a designer home in the Village of Poinciana, in a retirement community called The Villages. The Villages, located in Central Florida in Lake, Sumter, and Marion Counties, covers 32 square miles and is home to over 77,000 people over the age of 55. As a wonderful bonus, retired military make up more than a fifth of the population.

I've not seen such support for the military among the civilian population in my life. It makes me proud to be among so many warriors.

One of the nicest things that have happened to me since moving here is my participation in the Flightless Honor Flight.

Starting in 2011, veterans in the Villages fly to Washington DC to visit the memorial of the wars in which they served. The local chapter of Honor Flight is active and provides trips for veterans at no cost, four times each year. For those who cannot travel, the program offers a "Flightless Honor Flight," where veterans can enjoy a virtual flight.

The community shows its support for those who have served by providing a send-off and return gala at the local American Legion Hall. The cheerleading team, clown group, and other fun organizations gather wave flags and clap for each veteran. Blaring sirens, a police contingent, and The Villages Motorcycle club escort Honor Flight buses through towns on their way to Orlando Airport. People clap and cheer as the veterans walk through the airport where active duty service members greet them. Upon return, the fire department spays a welcome over their buses.

Being so honored brings a lump to my throat whenever I share my Photobook about my trip.

The best part of living in The Villages is the availability of golfing opportunities. Helen and I play golf several times each week. There are over fifty golf courses available to residents. The weather is super. When not golfing, there are concerts, card games, and other activities possible. People help each other. There are many medical clinics and a large Veteran's Association.

The Tri-County Women Veterans Group meets once each month at one of the country clubs in The Villages. Over one-hundred female veterans from every branch of the service attend. We share companionship and work together to support various organizations. My military life has come full circle with this organization.

Awards Ribbons Honors

Trailblazer Firsts

1. Created the first Navy Family Services Program.
2. Created the first Transition Office helping servicemen returning from Vietnam
3. First female naval officer selected for post-graduate work at a civilian university
4. First female instructor at Industrial College of the Armed Forces
5. Wrote recommendations adapting ships for female sailors.
6. Member of the DACOWITS recommending easing restrictions of women serving in the Navy.
7. The Defense Meritorious Service Medal
8. The National Defense Service Medal
9. Two Navy Legion of Merit Medals

Doris Vail

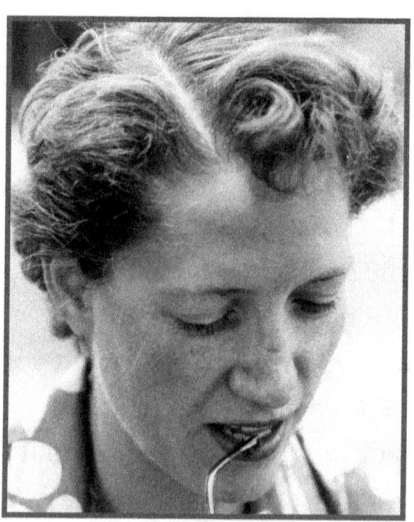

Doris Vail, a student at University of Denver, contemplating the future.

Doris Vail
About the Author

Born in Loveland, Colorado, in 1935, Doris moved with her family to Cheyenne, Wyoming, where, at five years old, she became ill and spent time in The Children's Hospital in Denver. After three years, Doris returned to her family in Cheyenne, where she attended school. Miss Vail graduated with a degree in special education from The University of Denver and enrolled in the Navy in 1958. She tells her story of serving in the United States Navy.

As a trailblazer, Doris served as the first female officer in several positions held traditionally by men. She was involved in official committees and wrote regulations exploring how the Navy can better accommodate the increasing involvement of women in non-traditional jobs.

While in the service, Doris attended different schools as the first Naval woman earning her master's degree in personnel administration. She continued her education, earning her DBA in business administration. Upon retirement, Doris continued aiding other female veterans.

Her parents worked in Cheyenne, Wyoming, until

Doris Vail

retirement in 1970. Her father, Donald B. Vail, worked as a switchman on the Union Pacific Railroad, while her mother, Dorothy Vail, worked in the Wyoming Land Office. Her brother, Dexter Vail, served in the US Navy for three years, then became a technician on radar and landing gear gadgets. Her sister, Donna, married and raised five children.

Doris lives in The Villages, Florida.

ACKNOWLEDGMENTS

I wish to thank Margaret Best for her help as my assistant, editor, and ghostwriter. A special thank you goes to Helen Hardbower for her support and computer knowledge in writing this book. Without encouragement from the Tri-County Women Veterans of The Villages, Florida, this book may not have been written.

References

1. Interviews with Doris
2. Collins, Craig. Making Waves. Women in the U.S. Navy. March 27, 2018.
3. CNN Staff "By the Numbers: Women in the U.S. military" Jan. 24, 2013. https://www.cfr.org/article/demographic-us-military
4. Dev, Mary "With Historic Number of Women in Uniform the Vet Community is About to Change" March 11, 2018, http://www.military.com/daily-news/2019/03/11/history-number-women-uniform-vet-community-about-change.hyml
5. Fleet & Family Readiness, Pamphlet Commander Navy Installations Command 716 Sicard Street St. Suite 1000 Washington D.C. 20374
6. U.S. Dept of Defense. " For You an Officer's Career in the U.S. Armed Forces" January 1, 1966. Pamphlet.
7. Gjenvick-Gjonvik Archives 2158 Wilmington Circle NE Marietta GA 30062 https://www.gjenvick.com/Military/NavyArchives/USNTC/Year/1962-BootCampBooks.html
8. Nakeshima, Ellen "In Praise of Women Who Served" The Washington Post June 23, 1995
9. Navy Archives "1970s Family Policy The Women's Memorial" https://www.womensmemorial.org/history/detail/?s=1970s-family-policy
10. Rank Insignia of Navy Commissioned and Warrant Officers. August 2009 https://www.navy.mil/navydata/ranks/officers/o-rank.hyml
11. United States History. WAVES https://u-s-history.com/pages/h1708.html
12. Welcome to Naval Base San Diego https://www.cnic.navy.mil/regions/cnrsw/installations/nav-base-san-diego.html
13. Women In The Navy. Half-Century Chronology http://www.phs.org/wgbh/pages/frontline/shows/navy/plus/cron.html
14. https://www.globalsecurity.org/military/facility/broadway.htm Chapter 3 Navy Broadway Complex San Diego
15. Facilities Women's Memorial Washington DC The Women in Military Service of America Memorial
16. Z-gram #116; Dated 7 August 1972 Equal Rights and Opportunities for Women August 1972 17.
17. Zumwalt, Elmo R. Jr. https://www.history.navy.mi/browse-by-topic/people/chiefs-os-navel-operations/admiral-elm-r-zumwalt-legacy.html Oct. 7, 2016.

www.ingramcontent.com/pod-product-compliance
Lightning Source LLC
LaVergne TN
LVHW052340080426
835508LV00045B/3068